T0145053

THE
BASEBALL
BAT

A True Story

WILF PAULS

WestBow Press books may be ordered through booksellers or by contacting:

WestBow Press
A Division of Thomas Nelson & Zondervan
1663 Liberty Drive
Bloomington, IN 47403
www.westbowpress.com
844-714-3454

ISBN: 979-8-3850-0185-9 (sc)
ISBN: 979-8-3850-0186-6 (hc)
ISBN: 979-8-3850-0187-3 (e)

Library of Congress Control Number: 2023912115

Print information available on the last page.

WestBow Press rev. date: 7/26/2023

WESTBOW
PRESS®
A DIVISION OF THOMAS NELSON
& ZONDERVAN

To Reuben, Scott, Erich, and Jacob—
Baseball brothers,
Men of integrity

Acknowledgments

It has been an incredible privilege to work with the following enthusiastic supporters of this project. Your creative participation and patience, as you acted out your role during the photo sessions, were a delight.

Our grandson Hudson is Wilf, age seven.

Bryce, another grandson, is my brother Reuben, age ten.

Olivia, our granddaughter, is my sister Olive, age eleven.

Seija, our daughter, acts as my mother. She is also mom to Hudson and Olivia.

Roxanne Sewell, Hudson's grade one teacher, and Brady Holland, Hudson and Olivia's principal, gave life to the school connection. Thank you.

Joel Feddersen, pastor of Metro Community Church—thank you for being You.

A special thanks to David Emond for the grand finale photo at the end of the story.

Pearl, my wife, who took a chance by marrying a former thief with a secret, has never wavered in the telling of this story. For her valued insights and questions, I am truly grateful.

Thank you to each of you, as well as the rest of our family and friends, for your honest input and encouragement.

Prologue

In April 1958, our family moved from a small farm in Saskatchewan to Kelowna, British Columbia, Canada. We were very poor. A 1953 GMC truck carried our parents and four children, all packed into the crowded cab. Dad earned $1.50 per hour building houses. Our rent was $70 per month. In the summer of 1958, we moved out of town to a dilapidated, filthy house with no running water. It was close to a property where my dad could build a new house. As soon as the roof was on and the walls were up, we moved into the unfinished house.

This story begins at Gordon Road Elementary School in Kelowna, which is still being used as the Justice Institute of British Columbia. We took the first twelve photos here. There is no baseball backstop anymore, but the soccer field is still in use.

The old rental house is gone, so we couldn't use it in the book. I found an old house that looked like the shack we moved into part way into the story.

The baseball bat is not the original one for a reason you will discover as you read the story!

All the characters are real. My brother, Reuben, really was my best friend as we grew up. We always wanted to be on the same team. Even as adults, we played ball together. Our friendship continues to this day.

On the last page of the story, I am standing beside my seven-year-old grandson, Hudson, who is the same age as I was in the story.

Wow! I couldn't believe my eyes! A beautiful baseball bat, the perfect size, was lying at home plate on the ball diamond farthest from the school.

Our bat at home was embarrassing. You got slivers if you picked it up the wrong way. My family was too poor for me to ask for a new bat.

Ever since I was four years old, my brother and I had taken turns pitching and hitting the ball with that ugly old stick. We loved baseball!

Now here in front of me was a treasure.

I put down my lunch bag and picked up the bat. No slivers! It was smooth. I checked the trademark, stepped up to the plate, and got ready for the pitch.

I swung with all my seven–year–old strength. Home run! I felt like a champion.

As I looked across the field to the playground, the parking lot, and the school, I realized that I was alone; there was not a single person in sight. My brother, Reuben, would certainly be impressed if I brought a bat home. Should I just take it?

It wasn't my fault that someone had left it out there all afternoon. Was it my job to bring it back to the school? If I left it there overnight, someone else might take it. But there was no one else. Why was I thinking these things? I put the bat down, picked up the lunch bag, and walked to the street.

I stopped on the road and looked back at the bat lying there. Oh, how I wanted that amazing bat! Maybe the bat was really mine because I found it. It wasn't really stealing; it was finding. Finders keepers, losers weepers, right?

I knew I should just go home. But I didn't. I went back to home plate and picked up the nicest bat in the world. I ran my fingers up and down its length and took a few more swings. I looked around. Still, no one was on the school grounds. No one was on the road. No one was outside in their yard.

If I tucked the handle under my armpit and held the bat against my leg, would anyone see an innocent little kid taking it from the school grounds? I felt nervous. Why was I scared? I had found it, and it was OK to find things, right? If someone yelled at me, I could drop it and run. *OK, I'll do it*, I thought.

I took one more good look around, and then I walked off the ballfield as naturally as possible. My heart pounded like a jackhammer. And then I was on the road. *Don't look back. Just keep walking*, I thought.

I was free. Not one person had stopped me, asked me what I was doing, or even seen me! I had found a bat; that's what I would tell my brother. I didn't want to tell a lie. I just wouldn't say where I had found it on the way home from school.

And then I saw something that stopped me in my tracks: the letters GRE on the knob of the bat.

Oh no! Gordon Road Elementary. My family would know. I'd be caught for sure!

How could I erase those dark letters? I kicked a rock. That's it! Gravel! I put the knob on the ground, held the barrel with both hands, and scraped the bat back and forth as hard as I could. I checked the end, but there was still too much black ink. I leaned on the bat harder. Finally, after four scrubbings, the bat was scuffed, but it was clean.

Whew! I could hardly wait to get home. I ran into the yard yelling, "Look what I found! Look what I found!"

Reuben came running. I handed him the bat. He took a few swings. "Wow! That's a great bat!" He ran to the kitchen window, held up the bat, and said, "Mom, look at this bat! Wilf found it!" Mom smiled.

"Where did you find it?" she asked. "He found it on the way home from school," Reuben answered for me. "But where was it?" Mom prodded. "Just lying on the ground," I answered truthfully. And that was it. I'd passed the test. No more questions. I was a hero!

We played ball till Mom called us for dinner.

Then we played more after the dishes were done. Olive joined us.

Reuben, my best friend, was proud of me, his little brother. I smiled as I lay in my bed that evening.

But then it hit me. Tomorrow morning, I had to go to school. Suddenly I was scared.

Maybe I should take it back and just drop the bat on the ballfield. But I couldn't. What would Reuben or the rest of my family say if they knew the truth? They wouldn't trust me anymore.

I felt stuck. I felt sick. I didn't sleep well.

The next morning, I slowly shuffled my way to school. Would my teacher know? What about the principal? I felt like a criminal. But my teacher welcomed me. The bell rang, and another day started.

Just before recess, there was a knock at the door. It was the principal. My heart felt like a jackhammer again. He looked around the classroom. I wanted to shrink into my desk. He talked with the teacher, glanced at me, and walked away. Did he know something? My stomach was in knots.

The rest of the day was like a dream. None of the older kids talked about a missing bat. The principal didn't come back. When I got home, no one said the school had called. Yahoo! I wanted to scream. Nobody knew my secret! Nobody knew that the new boy in grade one had stolen a bat. A heavy load slid off my back.

We played a lot of ball in May and June, but for some reason, I was still bothered by what I had done. I was the only person in the whole world who knew the true story, and yet I couldn't get it out of my head. And then in July, we moved again. Good. Another school. Now my secret was completely safe.

An old shack was our temporary home while Dad and Mom built a new house.

As we unpacked our bags and boxes in that dilapidated place, I kept looking for my bat. Where was it? Maybe someone had stolen it. "Don't worry; we'll find it," everyone told me. But we never did. The bat was lost forever.

At first, I felt cheated. It wasn't fair. It was such a cool bat! But then I thought, *That bat still bothered me every time I played with it. Why?* Maybe if I didn't have it anymore, I'd feel better.

The bat was gone. I was free. But not really—I still knew the truth. Every time I played ball, I knew. Sometimes I'd forget, but at night that bat felt so heavy again.

I went through grades two, three, four, and into five. I was pitching for the school team. But often, when I held a bat, I still remembered that dreadful day in grade one. Why had I done it? Why had I ever picked it up? Why didn't I just bring it back? I hated that bat. Everyone thought I was such a good, honest boy. I couldn't tell anyone. People would think I was a bad person.

One Sunday in church, the pastor said that if we asked God to forgive all the wrong things we'd ever done, He'd do it. *Yes!* I thought. *I won't have to tell anyone else!*

But then he went on to say, "Sometimes, if we can, we need to make things right with the people we have wronged."

Oh no! That was the worst part. How could I ever do that?

I passed to grade six. I had lots of friends and played other sports, like soccer, hockey, and table tennis. But playing baseball, especially with Reuben, was my favourite.

I still felt guilty about the bat. Then one day in July, a simple yet amazing idea exploded in my mind. I knew I had the answer! Why hadn't I thought of it before? I could do this. Yes!

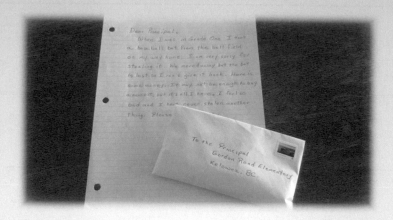

I found an envelope and a stamp and closed the door of my bedroom. I collected all the money I had saved, and then I wrote a letter. "Dear Principal …" I told him about stealing the bat and losing the bat and how sorry I was and that I'd learned a hard lesson and how maybe this wasn't enough money for a new one, but it was all I had. On the envelope I wrote, "To the Principal, Gordon Road Elementary School."

I dropped the letter with all those coins into the mail slot. *Clunk!* It sounded wonderful. I didn't care if anyone saw me. That heavy backpack of guilt dropped from my shoulders.

Do you know what happy feels like? Both of my arms shot up as I leaped into the air and shouted! The sun was brighter. My body felt lighter. I'd never been happier. I was finally free! Free to be me honestly!

Hudson and Wilf

The End

Do children in grade one know what stealing and lying are? How many ways did the boy use in the story to try to hide his actions?

It was the first time this boy had stolen something. His parents had taught the whole family the importance of honesty. Who taught him how to steal?

The boy could have returned the bat but chose not to. Why?

I worked in a country where anything left outside or unlocked was stolen. When the laundry was hung outside (there was no dryer), someone had to guard the clothes, or they would disappear. At the end of the day, my family also had to take down the washing line, or people would steal that as well. Another place was just the opposite. I could leave the large garage door wide open for a whole weekend when our family went on a trip, and nothing would ever be taken. In what kind of place do you live? Is there anything you would like to change?

In North America, one out of eleven people have shoplifted. One-quarter of them are children. Most people don't plan to steal ahead of time. I didn't wake up that morning with the plan to steal a baseball bat. Have you ever taken something that didn't belong to you? Have you ever been caught? How did you feel? Maybe you never have been caught? How do you feel?

What about people who don't feel guilty—people who think it's cute or funny? What would you say to them? My approach is to ask them how they feel when someone steals something they value. We all need to realize that when a person steals, someone else loses something. My school lost a good baseball bat.

Anyone can make a poor choice. The good news is that we can try to make it right. You can say, "I'm sorry." You can try to repay or replace something you stole, if possible. It is a great relief to talk with someone who understands. Have you ever had this experience?

WILF PAULS

Wilf Pauls
#107-1885 Parkview Cres.
Kelowna, BC, Canada
V1X 7E2
Email: wilfpauls@gmail.com
Telephone: 250-860-0161

Printed in the United States
by Baker & Taylor Publisher Services